LIGHTHOUSES

SEAN FINNIGAN

TABLE OF CONTENTS

Lighthouses are built near water on islands and beaches. They help **guide** ships at night, or when it is hard to see because of fog or storms.

A lighthouse can help guide a ship along dangerous coastlines where there are rocks or the water is shallow.

Long ago, people built fires on hilltops to help warn ships of dangerous coastlines.

A lighthouse called
the Pharos of Alexandria
in Egypt may have been
the first lighthouse ever built.
It was built between 300 and
280 B.C., and was destroyed
by **invaders** and earthquakes
over many years.

The oldest lighthouse
still standing is in Spain.
It was built
around 20 A.D.

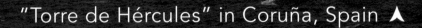
"Torre de Hércules" in Coruña, Spain ⋀

Early lighthouses had lamps that were lit using vegetable oil or whale blubber. The beam from these lamps could only be seen for a few miles.

▲ Today, working lighthouses use electricity.

A lighthouse keeper
took care of the lighthouse.
The keeper would trim
the **wick**, refill the oil,
clean the lamps, as well as dust
and paint the lighthouse.

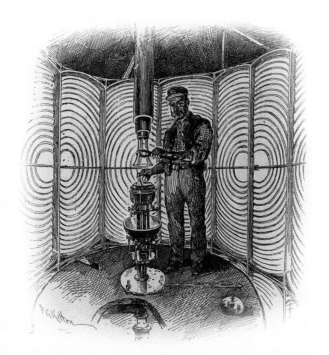

In 1822, the first modern **lens** was invented by Augustin Fresnel. He discovered that you could increase light by using **prisms**. In 1841, the first Fresnel lens was put into a lighthouse in Europe.

The Fresnel lens is still used in many lighthouses.
The lens can be as tall as 12 feet.

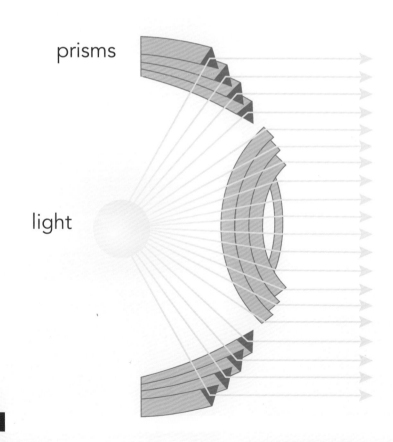

prisms

light

There are many lighthouses on the coastlines and on large lakes of the United States. The first U.S. lighthouse was built on Brewster Island in Boston, Massachusetts in 1716.

The original tower
was destroyed by the British
during the Revolutionary War.
A new lighthouse was built
in its place in 1784.

The oldest lighthouse
still standing in the United States
is in Sandy Hook, NJ.
It was built in 1764.

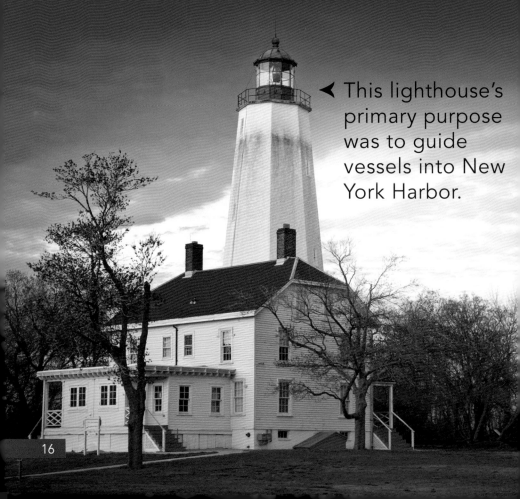

◄ This lighthouse's primary purpose was to guide vessels into New York Harbor.

The tallest lighthouse
in the United States
is in Cape Hatteras, NC.
It is 196 feet tall.
It was built in 1872.

➤ The light from this lighthouse
can be seen 20-miles out to
sea. It has warned sailors for
more than 100 years of the
shallow sandbars near Cape
Hatteras, North Carolina.

Today lighthouses play a less important role in navigation than they did years ago. Modern lighthouses no longer need a lighthouse keeper. Lighthouses today mostly use solar-charged batteries and have a single flashing light.

Over the years, many lighthouses have fallen into **disrepair**. Some lighthouses have been **restored.** You can visit these lighthouses and learn about their history.

Here is the lighthouse in St Augustine, Florida. This lighthouse is located in the oldest port in the Unites States. Visitors can visit the light keepers houses, and climb the 219 steps to the top of the lighthouse!

GLOSSARY

disrepair: something neglected and needing repair

guide: to assist while traveling

invaders: to enter forcefully as an enemy

lens: glass used to help vision

prisms: often triangular in shape and used to disperse light

restored: to bring back to original state

wick: a soft thread used to light candles or oil lights

INDEX